The Ecumenical Patriarchate

A Brief Guide

The Ecumenical Patriarchate

A Brief Guide

Fr. John Chryssavgis

The Order of St. Andrew the Apostle
Archons of the Ecumenical Patriarchate

The Ecumenical Patriarchate
A Brief Guide
Fr. John Chryssavgis

© The Order of St. Andrew the Apostle, Inc., 2004
8 East 79th Street, New York, NY 10021 U.S.A.
Tel. (212) 570 3550 Fax: (212) 774 0214
www.archons.org

Third Edition, 2009

Edited by
Brian Johnson - Paul Gikas

Photographs
Gültekin Tetik
Nikolaos Manginas (pp. 8, 58–79)

Designed by
Murat Celep
Deney Tasarım Ltd.

Printed and bound by
Ofset Yapımevi
Yahya Kemal Mah. Şair Sok. No: 4 Kağıthane - İstanbul

ISBN-10: 0-9787270-0-2
ISBN-13: 978-0-9787270-0-0
Library of Congress Control Number: 2006929153

Front cover illustration: Mosaic depicting St. Andrew the Apostle (left), founder of the Church of Constantinople, handing the Holy Gospel to his disciple and successor,
St. Stachys, the first bishop of the city of Byzantium.

Title page illustration: The Patriarchal Church of Saint George (east facade).

The Ecumenical Patriarchate
Fatih - Haliç 34220
Istanbul, Turkey
Tel. +90 212 531 96 70–76
Fax: +90 212 531 65 33
www.patriarchate.org

This guidebook is dedicated to His All Holiness Bartholomew, Archbishop of Constantinople, New Rome and Ecumenical Patriarch for his extraordinary spiritual leadership and worldwide ministry.

National Council
Order of St. Andrew
Archons of the Ecumenical Patriarchate in America
2004

Contents

His All Holiness Ecumenical Patriarch Bartholomew I.

Foreword

This book was conceived, developed and commissioned by the Order of St. Andrew/Archons of the Ecumenical Patriarchate in America to serve as an educational instrument to enlighten visiting pilgrims to Istanbul regarding the extraordinary architectural, iconographic and theological treasures that exist at the Ecumenical Patriarchate.

This third edition includes milestone events that have taken place at the Spiritual Center of World Orthodoxy including the 2004 Return of the Relics of St. Gregory the Theologian and St. John Chrysostom; the 2006 Papal Visit to the Phanar; the 2008 Synaxis of the Heads of the Orthodox Churches chaired by His All Holiness Ecumenical Patriarch Bartholomew and the Symposium of St. Paul commemorating the 2000th Anniversary of the Ministry of St. Paul traveling in cities of Turkey and Greece where St. Paul preached during his missionary journeys.

The Order of St. Andrew is an organization of leading Orthodox churchmen in America who promote the well-being of the Ecumenical Patriarchate, the spiritual center of 300 million Orthodox faithful throughout the world. Archons historically were the leading citizens of the Roman/Byzantine Empire, which existed for a millennium until the Fall of Constantinople on Tuesday, May 29, 1453. Today, the Archons of America, whose ranks include members of Congress, government leaders, successful businessmen and exemplary stewards of the Orthodox Church, devote themselves to *Defending the Faith* and serving the needs of the Ecumenical Patriarchate.

Order of St. Andrew the Apostle
Archons of the Ecumenical Patriarchate in America
2009
www.archons.org

The Orthodox Church

The Orthodox Church numbers some 300 million people worldwide. Geographically, its primary area of distribution lies in Eastern and Northern Europe, along the coast of the (northeastern) Mediterranean and in the Middle East. It is composed of several self-governing or Patriarchal Churches, a form of international federation within which each local Church retains its independence while remaining committed to unity in faith and worship.

The term "Orthodox" was first adopted in the early fourth-century Christian Church by the Greek fathers in order to determine and distinguish the canonical faith from heterodox, or heretical, doctrines and deviations. Today, it forms part of the official title of the Eastern Church and those in communion with it. Also included in the title are certain other Churches of the East, which were separated in the fifth century as a result of the Monophysite controversy over the question of Christ's two natures.

The hierarchy and administration of the Orthodox Church is based on the ancient orders of bishop, presbyter (priest), and deacon.[1] Each diocese has integrity as the full expression of the Church, while maintaining full communion and unity of faith with every other diocese. Many people tend to think of the Church as a vast, worldwide institution. Yet the concept of universality, or catholicity, as expressed in the local community, is a fundamental aspect of Orthodox theology and tradition, which recognizes each local Eucharistic gathering as related on the principle of identity and as reflecting the fullness of the Body of Christ.

As a result of this vision of the Church, or ecclesiology, one may refer to the Orthodox Church as well as to the Orthodox Churches. In this "one Body of Christ" comprising "many parts," the Ecumenical Patriarchate serves as the "first among equals," as Mother Church to a family of local Churches throughout the world.

---

[1] There are a number of titles and positions within the hierarchy of the Orthodox Church but all of them fall under one of these fundamental three orders. For instance, a grand archdeacon is a deacon; an archimandrite is a priest; and every metropolitan, archbishop and patriarch (even the Ecumenical Patriarch) is a bishop—although each of these has a distinct spiritual responsibility, administrative role, or jurisdictional authority.

The Pentarchy—the five ancient Patriarchates.

The title "Patriarch" is adopted for the head of various Orthodox Churches. Originally confined to the five ancient Churches of Rome, Constantinople, Alexandria, Antioch, and Jerusalem—the "Pentarchy," or five ruling Churches, officially codified under Emperor Justinian (527–565)—the title was later extended to the Metropolitan of Moscow in the sixteenth century, to the Archbishops of Serbia and Bulgaria in the early twentieth century, as well as to the head of the Romanian Church in the middle of the twentieth century. The ancient Church of Georgia rejoices in the title "Catholicos."

Theology and Spirituality

The Orthodox Church is characterized by a profound sense of continuity with the Apostolic Church, adhering to the faith and practices defined by the first seven Ecumenical Councils. The word "Orthodox" signifies both "right believing" and "right worshipping," and so the Orthodox Church is recognized as the bearer of an uninterrupted living tradition of true faith lived out in worship.

The roots of the Church lie in Scripture and Tradition, as these are manifested in the life of the Church and the early Fathers. External criteria of truth are not foremost; Orthodox Christianity seeks the living experience of truth accessible in the Communion of Saints, wherein the Mother of God, or Theotokos, holds a special place of honor.

Venerated from the early cult of the martyrs, the saints are honored as witnesses to the fullness of the experience to which all baptized Christians are called and, as such, are considered intercessors for all Christians. They cover a range of professions and functions, reflected in their titles. For instance, St. George is known as a "Great Martyr" and as the "Trophy-Bearer." In most Orthodox cultures, the faithful are baptized with the name of a saint, celebrating the feast day of that saint in the place of a birthday.

For the Orthodox Church, the doctrine of the Holy Trinity underlies all theology and spirituality. Salvation is personal, implying particularity. Yet, salvation is also communal, implying sharing. It is on the teaching about the Holy Trinity that the conciliar and hierarchical structure of the Orthodox Church rests.

Furthermore, the mystery of the Trinity is revealed in the supreme act of divine love expressed through the incarnation of the Word of God that assumed flesh, embracing and healing all humanity that is called to become deified by grace and the entire creation that is called to transfiguration by divine energy.

Participation in the deified humanity of Jesus Christ is the ultimate goal of the Christian life, accomplished through the Holy Spirit in the sacramental life of the Church. The Orthodox Church experiences and expresses its

The beauty and splendor of Orthodox worship is reflected in a service in the Patriarchal Church of St. George.

theology in liturgy, which has in fact accounted for the survival of the Church in times of turmoil. It was the liturgical dimension of the Church that encouraged and educated Orthodox faithful during the four hundred years of Ottoman rule (1453–1821), as well as more recently during persecutions in post-revolutionary Russia.

Orthodox worship and spirituality appeal to all the senses. Therefore, icons, or sacred images, reflect a sense of beauty and glory, providing perhaps the most striking and most widely appreciated aspect of the Orthodox Church.[2] The distinctiveness and multitude of icons is the fruit of a long theological reflection unique to the Orthodox world. Icons are venerated, not worshipped. They are the faith depicted in color, constituting part of the transfigured cosmos. Since early Christian times, and especially since the Seventh Ecumenical Council of 787, sacred icons have provided specific affirmation of the doctrine of Divine Incarnation as well as general education in matters of faith. The end of a long controversy over icons in 843 is solemnly remembered each year on the first Sunday of Great Lent, also known as the Sunday of Orthodoxy.

Finally, the importance of apophatic (or negative) theology, underlining the mystery and transcendence of God even while affirming His presence and immanence, dictates a reluctance to define or pontificate on matters of ethical importance. The deeper conviction always is that truth can never be exhausted, while each human person is uniquely created in the image of God, never able to be reduced to anything less than a mystery.

---

[2] Orthodox Christians refer to both painted images and mosaics as icons.

The Ecumenical Patriarchate

The Ecumenical Patriarchate is the highest see and holiest center of the Orthodox Christian Church throughout the world. It is an institution with a history spanning seventeen centuries, during which it retained its see in Constantinople (present-day Istanbul). It constitutes the center of all the local Orthodox Churches, heading these not by administration but by virtue of its primacy in the ministry of pan-Orthodox unity and the coordination of the activity of the whole of Orthodoxy.

The grounds of the Ecumenical Patriarchate, showing the Evgenidio where the Patriarch's personal quarters are located.

The function of the Ecumenical Patriarchate as center *par excellence* of the life of the entire Orthodox world emanates from its centuries-old ministry in the witness, protection and outreach of the Orthodox faith. The Ecumenical Patriarchate therefore possesses a supra-national and supra-regional character. From this lofty consciousness and responsibility for the people of Christ, regardless of race and language, were born the new regional Churches of the East, from the Caspian to the Baltic, and from the Balkans to Central Europe. This activity today extends to the Far East, to America and Australia.

Orthodox Christians on all continents, which do not fall under the jurisdiction of the autocephalous (independent) or autonomous (semi-independent) Churches, fall under the direct jurisdiction of the Ecumenical Patriarchate. The most important of the autocephalous Churches are the ancient Patriarchates of Alexandria, Antioch and Jerusalem (together with the ancient Archdiocese of Mt. Sinai), the Patriarchates of Russia, Serbia, Romania, Bulgaria and Georgia, as well as the Churches of Cyprus, Greece, Poland, Albania, and the Church of the Czech Lands and Slovakia. The autonomous Churches include those of Finland and of Estonia. Consequently, the Orthodox Churches in Europe, America, Australia and Britain, which are not under the jurisdiction of the aforementioned autocephalous Churches, lie within the jurisdiction of the Ecumenical Patriarchate. All Orthodox feel that they are constituents of one essentially spiritual community, wherein "when one member suffers, so do all." It is a true sense of unity in diversity.

A surviving section
Constantinople's ancient w
built roughly a century af
the city became the capita
the Roman Empire in 3

History of the Ecumenical Patriarchate

Following the establishment of Constantinople (the ancient city of Byzantium) as the state capital of the Roman Empire in the early part of the fourth century, a series of significant ecclesiastical events saw the status of the Bishop of New Rome (as Constantinople was then called) elevated to its current position and privilege. The Church of Constantinople is traditionally regarded as being founded by St. Andrew, the "first-called" of the Apostles. The 3rd canon of the Second Ecumenical Council held in Constantinople (381) conferred upon the bishop of this city second rank after the Bishop of Rome. Less than a century later, the 28th canon of the Fourth Ecumenical Council held in Chalcedon (451) offered Constantinople equal ranking to Rome and special responsibilities throughout the rest of the world and expanding its jurisdiction to territories hitherto unclaimed.

St. Andrew the Apostole (left), founder of the Church of
Constantinople, hands the Holy Gospel to his disciple and successor,
St. Stachys, the first bishop of the city of Byzantium (mosaic panel
in the main entrance to the Patriarchal House).

The Ecumenical Patriarchate holds an honorary primacy among the autocephalous, or ecclesiastically independent, Churches. It enjoys the privilege of serving as "first among equals." It is also known as the "Roman" Patriarchate (hence the Turkish phrase: Rum Patrikhanesi), recalling its historical source as the Church of New Rome, the new capital of the Roman Empire, transferred in 330 from Old Rome to Byzantium by Constantine the Great. The first bishop of the city of Byzantium was St. Stachys (38–54), a disciple of the Apostle Andrew. In 330, Byzantium was renamed Constantinople and New Rome, while its bishopric was elevated to an archbishopric. The Metropolitan of Heraclea, to whom Byzantium was formerly subject, now came under the jurisdiction of Constantinople and enjoyed the privileges of the latter's most senior see.

As a title, the phrase "Ecumenical Patriarchate" dates from the sixth century and belongs exclusively to the Archbishop of Constantinople. The Great Schism of 1054—in fact the culmination of a gradual estrangement over many centuries—resulted in formal separation between the Churches of the East and the West, granting Constantinople sole authority and jurisdiction over the Orthodox Churches throughout the world.

After the capture of Constantinople by the Latins during the Fourth Crusade (1204), the Ecumenical Patriarchate was transferred to Nicaea (1206), but Emperor Michael VIII Palaeologos restored it to Constantinople when he recaptured the city in 1261. When Constantinople became the capital of the Ottoman Empire in 1453, the Ecumenical Patriarch (at the time, Gennadius II) was recognized as *Ethnarch* of the Orthodox peoples, with increased authority over the Eastern Patriarchates and the Balkan Churches, as well as farther afield.

From that time, the Ecumenical Patriarchate became a symbol of unity, rendering service and solidarity to the Eastern Churches. In difficult periods, the Ecumenical Patriarchate was consulted for the resolution of problems. Frequently, patriarchs of other Churches would reside in Constantinople, which was the venue for meetings of the Holy Synod that was chaired by the Ecumenical Patriarch.

The Ecumenical Patriarchate also sponsored missionary growth through the centuries, the most notable of which was the conversion of the Kievan Rus in the tenth century and the most recent of which was the missionary work in Southeast Asia in the last century. This pastoral role and responsibility has earned the characterization of the Ecumenical Patriarchate as "the golden beacon of Orthodoxy, preserving the unwaning brilliance of Christianity."

Currently, the Ecumenical Patriarchate is actively engaged in diverse ecclesiastical activities and ministries. It has historically proved to be a dynamic leader in the ecumenical movement, fully participating in the World Council of Churches from its inception, as well as in local ecumenical bodies, instituting and chairing bilateral theological dialogues with non-Orthodox Christians but also with other monotheistic faiths.

Sultan Mehmet the Conqueror (left) officially recognizes Patriarch Gennadius II as leader of the Orthodox peoples following the Ottoman capture of Constantinople in 1453 (mosaic panel in the main entrance to the Patriarchal House).

Ecumenical Patriarch Bartholomew I

Born Demetrios Archondonis in 1940 on the island of Imvros (today, Gökçeada, Turkey), and elected 270th successor to the 2000-year-old Church founded by St. Andrew as well as Archbishop of Constantinople, New Rome, and Ecumenical Patriarch, His All Holiness Barthlomew I presides among all Orthodox Primates as the spiritual leader of 300 million faithful.

As a citizen of Turkey, his personal experience provides him with a unique perspective on religious tolerance and interfaith dialogue. Ecumenical Patriarch Bartholomew has worked for reconciliation among Christian Churches and acquired an international reputation for environmental awareness and protection. He has worked to advance reconciliation among Catholic, Muslim and Orthodox communities, such as in former Yugoslavia, and is supportive of peace-building measures to diffuse global conflict in the region. He has also presided over the restoration of the autocephalous Church of Albania and the autonomous Church of Estonia, proving a constant source of spiritual and moral support to those traditionally Orthodox countries emerging from decades of wide-scale religious persecution behind the Iron Curtain.

The current Ecumenical Patriarch's roles as the primary spiritual leader of the Orthodox Christian world and a transnational figure of global significance continue to become more vital each day. He co-sponsored the Peace and Tolerance Conference in Istanbul (1994) bringing together Christians, Muslims and Jews. Most noted are his efforts in environmental awareness, which have earned him the title "Green Patriarch." These endeavors, together with his efforts to promote religious freedom and human rights, have placed him at the forefront as an apostle of love, peace and reconciliation, earning him the Congressional Gold Medal by the United States Congress in 1997.

After completing his undergraduate studies at the Theological School of Halki (1961), he pursued graduate studies at the Pontifical Oriental Institute of the Gregorian University in Rome, the Ecumenical Institute in Bossey, and the University of Munich. Ordained to the Diaconate in 1961 and to the priesthood in 1969, Ecumenical Patriarch Bartholomew served as personal secretary to his predecessor, the late Ecumenical Patriarch

His All Holiness Ecumenical Patriarch Bartholomew I, Archbishop of Constantinople a[...] New Rome.

Demetrios (1972–1991), and was elected Metropolitan of Philadelphia (1973) and, later, Metropolitan of Chalcedon (1990). His tenure has been characterized by inter-Orthodox cooperation, inter-Christian and interreligious dialogue, as well as by formal trips to other Orthodox countries seldom previously visited. He has exchanged official visitations and accepted numerous invitations with ecclesiastical and state dignitaries.

Ecumenical Patriarch Bartholomew I holds numerous honorary doctorates, from the universities of Athens and Thessaloniki (Greece), Georgetown and Yale (United States), Flinders and Manila (Australasia), London, Edinburgh and Louvain, as well as Moscow and Bucharest (Europe). He speaks Greek, Turkish, Italian, German, French, English and Latin.

The Patriarchal Church of St. George

The Church of St. George in the Phanar (Fener) is the fifth Patriarchal church in Constantinople and home to the Ecumenical Patriarchate since the fifteenth century. Prior to the Fall of Constantinople in 1453, the Patriarchal churches were:

- A church (underground cave) in Argyroupolis (Fındıklı), 38–144.
- The Church of the Holy Seven Children and the Holy Eleazar in Elaion (Salıpazar), 148–166.
- A church in Sykais (Galata) until 272.
- The pre-Constantine Church of St. Irene until 398, today in the first garden of Topkapi Palace.
- The pre-Justinian Church of St. Sophia, 398–537.
- Justinian's Church of St. Sophia, 537–1204.
- The Church of St. Sophia in Nicaea (İznik), 1204–1261.
- Justinian's Church of St. Sophia, 1261–1453.

Since the Fall of Constantinople in 1453, the Patriarchal churches have been:

- The Church of the Twelve Apostles (location of today's Fatih Mosque), 1453–1456.
- The Church of Panagia Pammakaristos (today's Fethiye Mosque), 1456–1587.
- The Church of the Virgin Mary of Vlahseraion in the Phanar, 1587–1597.
- The Church of St. Dimitrios in Xyloporta (Ayvansaray), 1597–1600.
- The Church of St. George in the Phanar, 1601–present.

The current Patriarchal Church of St. George formerly served as a convent for Orthodox nuns. When Patriarch Matthew II (1598–1601) converted it to the home of the Ecumenical Patriarchate toward the end of his tenure, the nuns transferred to another community and the Phanar has served as a community for monks and the Center of Orthodoxy to this day. Indeed, the Phanar is sometimes referred to as "The Great Monastery." Monasticism and ascetic spirituality play a vital role in the Orthodox Church. Monastics play a prophetic role in the Orthodox Church, providing a powerful source of prayer in a world of turmoil and serving as a reminder of the heavenly

kingdom, which Christians expect and anticipate. In this way, monks and nuns comprise a balance between worldly power and divine love. To this day, the site itself of the Ecumenical Patriarchate comprises a monastic brotherhood under the spiritual guidance of the Ecumenical Patriarch.

The Church of St. George was refurbished in 1614 by Patriarch Timothy II (1612–1620), as attested to by the inscription on the facade of the church over the main entrance. Destroyed by fire in 1720, the church was completely rebuilt by Patriarch Jeremiah III (1716–1726), as commemorated by the inscription over the right entrance door. The two major donors, Constantinos Kapoukechagias and Athanasios Kiourtsibasis, are also acknowledged there. During the same year, again in the tenure of Patriarch Jeremiah, the church was renovated and a dome was constructed. Later, the dome was destroyed and the church was once more repaired in its present form in 1836 by Patriarch Gregory VI (1835–1840).

Facade of the Patriarchal Church of St. George, home to the Ecumenical Patriarchate since 1601.

The Patriarchal Church of St. George is a basilica with three aisles. Under the present Patriarch Bartholomew, it has been restored to its former beauty and redecorated through the generosity of the Grand Benefactor of the Ecumenical Patriarchate, Panagiotis Angelopoulos and his family.

The Church of St. George retains the classical threefold division of the narthex (vestibule), the nave, and the altar area.[3] It also reflects the early sixth-century basilicas with three-aisles. The narthex contains the icons of

---

[3] While the original church of the convent had a dome, the present Church of St. George, fundamentally reconstructed in the eighteenth and nineteenth centuries, does not have a dome. After the Fall of Constantinople, Christian buildings could not be covered with prominent domes and church architecture resembled more the ancient style of the basilica. Most churches in this region, especially those constructed in the eighteenth and the mid-nineteenth centuries, replaced the dome with a medallion of Christ Pantokrator, or "Almighty/All-Ruling," on the ceiling.

The nave of the Church of St. George,
looking towards the iconostasis.

St. George, to whom the church is dedicated, and of the Prophet Elijah, or Elias, wearing fur clothing in commemoration of the furrier merchants that brought the water system to the Phanar. The nave is the central place of congregation for the faithful and of celebration of the liturgy, other than the altar itself. The church has particular stalls reserved for the Hierarchs of the Throne, as well as for visiting clergy and dignitaries. The traditional monastic arrangement of seating in the nave is of ebony wood.

Finally, a comment should be made on the dedication of the Patriarchal church to St. George. It is most fitting that the church of the Ecumenical Patriarchate remembers this Great Martyr. The dimension of martyrdom is a fundamental spiritual characteristic of Orthodox people and places. Persecutions and divisions have always marked the history of the Orthodox Church—not unlike the story of the early Christian Church. These have shaped Orthodox identity and Orthodox spirituality alike. Therefore, martyrdom has profoundly marked the life and culture of the Eastern Church. While it may not always appear to be a normal feature of Christian life, martyrdom is definitely a normative factor of the Eastern Christian way. Martyrdom—whether a "red martyrdom" of blood in the case of those who suffer, or a "white martyrdom" of conscience in the heart in the case of the monastics—is part and parcel of the Orthodox way of living and thinking.

St. George, Patron Saint of the Patriarchal Church, slaying a dragon (from an icon in the narthex of the Church of St. George).

Orthodox Architecture and Liturgy

There is a well-known legend about an embassy sent by Prince Vladimir to Constantinople in the latter part of the tenth century in order to see whether the Russian people should adopt the religion of the Byzantines. After attending worship in the Great Church of Hagia Sophia, the envoys are said to have reported their overwhelming experience in the following words recorded in the *Russian Primary Chronicle*: "We knew not whether we were in heaven or on earth, for surely there is no such splendor or beauty anywhere upon earth. We cannot describe it to you; we only know that God dwells there among people . . . . We cannot forget that beauty."

A traditional Orthodox church has three dimensions, often reflected by three distinct spatial areas. The basic structure itself of a traditional Orthodox church is a synthesis of two classical elements: the dome (used as early as the fourth century) and the basilica (the earliest and simplest example of church architecture, built from available regional materials such as wood, stone and brick). Nevertheless, an Orthodox church is integrally three-dimensional. The church has three clearly defined spaces, three definite architectural zones. The dome is reserved for the image of Christ (Pantokrator), the central feature that embraces and enlightens the entire building. The second space is the church proper (the nave, or *naos*), filled with images of the saints and martyrs, monks and married people alike, appearing almost to blend in with the congregation itself. Finally, in traditional Orthodox churches, the third zone is dedicated to the Virgin Mary (Theotokos).

Where there is a dome, it is circular in shape, symbolical of the eternal and uncircumscribable divinity, a line without beginning or end. The floor plan of the church proper is rectangular, an image of the defined and limited nature of this world with its clear demarcations, beginnings and ends. The apse in the middle holds together the upper and lower zones, belonging to both and yet also pertaining to neither, uniting both the heavenly and the earthly realms, while at the same time inviting people to reconcile Creator and creation in their own bodies and in their surrounding world. The Mother of God, depicted in the apse, assumes both spherical and rectangular shape. She is the personification of this vocation and reconciliation. Thus, the apse reveals the sign and presence of God piercing history and entering time. In traditional churches, the absence of many pews further breaks down the separation between heaven and earth. Any subsidiary vaults and structural extensions assume the shape of a cross, the ultimate symbol of reconciliation and transfiguration (especially from the sixth-century reign of Justinian).

The principal sections of a traditional Orthodox church.

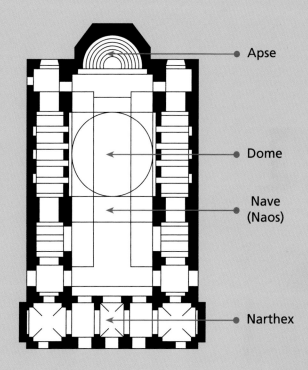

Apse

Dome

Nave (Naos)

Narthex

Beyond the sense of mystery, the significance of imagery, and the sensitivity to liturgy, perhaps the greatest contribution of Byzantine architecture is its flexibility. Orthodox architecture has endured the test of time, while also absorbing new techniques and building materials. It is at once traditional and original, always seeking to preserve the same essential dimensions. Byzantine architecture followed fixed formulas and rigid regulations, particularly after the tenth century when there were few if any new structural developments, with the exception perhaps of exterior decorations and the addition of bell-towers. While assuming cultural and regional stylistic variations, it bequeathed to subsequent generations an architectural beauty of countless variations on the same theme.

It is an art and an architecture that are aptly summed up in the Greek word *philokalia* ("love of the beautiful"). It is a living tradition that, at least in its more genuine expressions, seeks to retain a delicate balance between the aesthetic and the ascetic, between beauty and simplicity, in the fragility and vulnerability of the material and ephemeral.

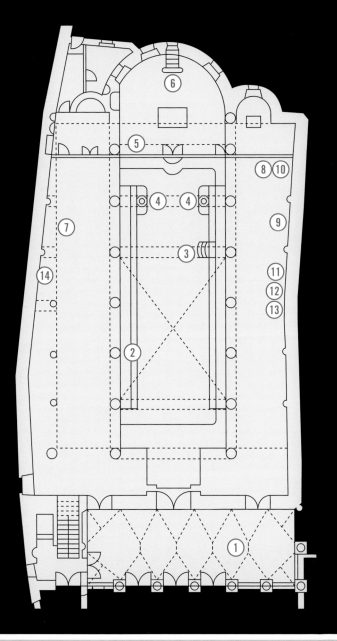

Apostolos Poridis

Plan of the Church of St. George

1. Candle Stand
2. Pulpit
3. Patriarchal Throne
4. Cantor's Stalls
5. Iconostasis
6. Synthronon
7. Icon of Panagia Faneromeni
8. Icon of St. John the Forerunner
9. Icon of Panagia Pammakaristos
10. Column of Flagellation
11. Relics of St. Theophano
12. Relics of St. Euphemia
13. Relics of St. Solomone
14. The Relics of St. Gregory the Theologian and St. John Chrysostom

A Tour of the Church of St. George

The Candle Stand (1)
The first thing that every Orthodox Christian will do upon entering a church is to kiss an icon and, then, light a candle. A symbol of the light of Christ, this candle will be placed alongside other candles in a special stand, a symbol of the community that characterizes the Body of Christ.

The candle stand on the right side of the narthex of the Church of St. George is the center of profound prayer and daily devotion. Constructed out of walnut and decorated with large ivory petals in the shape of a pentagon, this seventeenth-century candle stand is a replica of early Egyptian craftsmanship. The inscription cites that it was a gift by "Manuel, son of Peter, from Kastoria, donated in the year 1669."

The pulpit in
the Church of St. George.

The Pulpit (2)
Wrapped around a column on the left side of the nave, the pulpit is attributed by legend to the most famous preacher of the early Christian Church, St. John Chrysostom (347–407), who preached many historical sermons during his tenure as Patriarch of Constantinople. St. John was renowned for his inspired homilies; hence his epithet "Chrysostomos," which means "the golden-mouthed." Nevertheless, an inscription inside the pulpit states that it was constructed during the tenure of Gabriel III (1702–1707). The pulpit is made of walnut and mother of pearl and is decorated with the motif of a vine. Though simpler, its craftsmanship resembles that of the Patriarchal Throne.

The Patriarchal Throne (3)

The Patriarchal Throne in the middle of the nave is one of the most precious and valuable artifacts of the Church of St. George. Legend attributes the throne to the renowned Patriarch of Constantinople in the fourth century, St. John Chrysostom (398–404). According to the inscriptions beneath the eaves of the throne's gables, it was a gift offered in 1577 by Patriarch Jeremiah II to the Patriarchal Church of Panagia Pammakaristos. An inscription at the base of the throne recognizes it as the craftsmanship of an Athenian artist, Laurentios.

The throne stands four meters tall and is made of walnut. It is inlaid with ivory, mother of pearl and colored wood, fashioned in the form of a vine. In the past, it was also decorated with precious stones, but these are no longer there.

According to a third inscription, on one of the gables over its eaves, the throne was damaged between 1652 and 1654 during the tenure of Patriarch Paisios I (1652–1653, and 1654–1655). It was renovated by Patriarch Iakovos (1679–1682). The damage probably caused the loss of numerous gems as well as two icons, which formerly decorated the throne. These two icons were: a) Christ the Pantokrator, or "All Ruler"; and b) the Descent into Hades and Burial of Christ. The latter icon is described by Malaxos in 1577; its exact position on the throne remains unknown. The present icon on the throne also depicts Christ the Pantokrator; it is not the original icon, but a replacement icon commissioned by Patriarch Paisios I.

The proper throne of the Ecumenical Patriarch is in fact the *synthronon* (see below). The prominent Patriarchal Throne in the middle of the nave is the traditional seat of the abbot. The Patriarch, therefore, sits here as head of the monastic brotherhood, of "The Great Monastery," and may invite other, or visiting, hierarchs to officiate from this throne. On the two annual feasts of St. John Chrysostom—the commemoration of his repose on November 13 and the celebration of the transfer of his relics on January 27—the icon of St. John Chrysostom is placed on this throne, together with an episcopal staff, as though the Saint were presiding. On those days, the Ecumenical Patriarch is seated at the side-throne, or *parathronion*.

The Cantor's Stalls (4)

Used by the cantors of the Ecumenical Patriarchate, the two stalls in front of the iconostasis are among the artifacts transferred in 1942 to the Phanar from the (former) Holy Convent of Panagia Kamariotissa (or Koumariotissa) on the island of Halki. This island, well-known for its theological school, also housed the Palmons Commercial School. The stands, made of walnut and decorated with ivory, were renovated in 1947, as attested to by an inscription on the base of the left stall.

Exquisitely crafted, the Patriarchal Throne is attributed to St. John Chrysostom, Patriarch of Constantinople in the fourth century.

The iconostasis of the Church of St. George combines Byzantine, Renaissance, Baroque, and Ottoman artistic styles. Its extraordinary brilliance is the result of a restoration and gilding in 1994.

In the tradition of the Ecumenical Patriarchate, the style of chanting in the Church of St. George is unique, conveying at once a sense of triumphant glory and prayerful simplicity.

The Iconostasis (5)

The screen of icons separating the nave from the altar space is known as the iconostasis (or *templon*), which may range from a low, but ornate railing to a full wall, ceiling to floor, normally depicting scenes form the life of Christ, the martyrs, and the saints.[4] The icon screen of the Church of St. George does not adhere to any specific iconographic style, resembling more a conglomeration of Byzantine and Renaissance, as well as Baroque and even Ottoman influence. It is carved out of wood, which was recently gilded. The icon screen is divided into three sections and three levels. Smaller icons are placed before the icon screen itself in order to render them more accessible for personal devotion and veneration.

The middle section of icons contains the Royal Doors in the center, with two small icons depicting the Annunciation (the Archangel Gabriel and the Theotokos on the top panels); the two small icons on the lower panels depict the renowned Archbishops of Constantinople, St. Gregory the Theologian (329–389) and St. John Chrysostom (c. 347–407).[5] As visitors gaze at the icon screen, the right hand of the Royal Doors[6] is the traditional position for the icon of Christ, in this case Christ enthroned as the Great High Priest and pictured as the "True Vine." The traditional place for the icon of the Virgin Mother, or Theotokos, is on the left hand side of the Royal Doors. She is depicted here as the "Tree of Jesse," manifesting the generations prior to the birth of Christ. Other traditional positions of icons include the depiction of St. John the Baptist, or Forerunner (normally beside the icon of Christ), as well as the icon of the saint or feast to which the church is dedicated (normally beside the icon of the Virgin Mother), in this case the icon of St. George the Great Martyr.

---

[4] In other parts of the church, certain icons also contain biographical miniatures of the saint depicted, as in the icons of St. George, St. Nicholas, and St. Spyridon.

[5] Relics of these two Saints were returned to the Ecumenical Patriarchate from the Vatican at the initiative of Ecumenical Patriarch Bartholomew I in November 2004.

[6] The small gates opening from the iconostasis into the altar contain the symbolical double-headed eagle, a sign reminiscent of the close relationship between Church and State in the Byzantine Empire. Later theological interpretation attributes the two natures of Christ, divine and human, to this symbol. The same symbol is prominent on the facade of the Patriarchal church and elsewhere. Formerly an emblem of the Byzantine Empire, it now serves as an emblem of the ecumenical breadth—east and west, even as the eagle looks in both directions—of the Ecumenical Throne.

The northern (or left-hand) section[7] is a chapel dedicated to the Three Hierarchs (St. Basil the Great, St. John Chrysostom and St. Gregory the Theologian, whose joint feast is commemorated on January 30). On the right side of the smaller gate, there is an icon of the Virgin Mother holding Christ and an icon of St. Nicholas. On the left side, there is an icon of the Three Hierarchs and a full-length icon of the Archangel Michael (traditionally also the northern door to the altar).

The southern (or right-hand) section is a chapel dedicated to the Supplication of Panagia Pammakaristos. On the right side of the smaller gate, there is a mosaic of St. John the Baptist and an icon of St. Euphemia. On the left side, there is an icon of the two Great Martyrs, St. George and St. Demetrios, as well as an icon of the Archangel Michael[8] (traditionally also the southern door to the altar).

The two higher levels of icons include smaller panels depicting scenes and feasts from the New Testament (and especially the life of Christ) and the Old Testament (and especially from the life of the Prophets). They traditionally also depict the twelve Apostles of the Lord and the twelve major feast days of the Church.[9] These icon panels are lowered for veneration on certain feast days.

The Synthronon (6)
Located within the holy sanctuary on the other side of the iconostasis, behind the Holy Altar table, the *synthronon* consists of an elevated marble throne surrounded by eleven smaller, wooden thrones. According to canonical and liturgical tradition, only the Patriarch may be seated on the marble throne, while the other thrones are reserved for bishops of the Holy and Patriarchal Synod. This is in fact the proper throne of the Ecumenical Patriarch. And, since some of the marble on the *synthronon* dates back to the early fifth century, it may well have been graced by the presence of St. John Chrysostom.

The *synthronon* is an ancient liturgical practice of the Christian Church, symbolizing the unity of the faithful around the local bishop, who serves

---

[7] Architecturally, Orthodox churches traditionally face eastward, symbolical of the expectation and anticipation of the rising of the Sun of Righteousness, the Son of God, namely Jesus Christ.
[8] The Patriarchal church is unique in this regard, having two icons of the Archangel Michael. Normally, one side of the icon screen (traditionally, the northern door) depicts the Archangel Gabriel, while the other side (traditionally, the southern door) depicts the Archangel Michael.
[9] In the Patriarchal church, there appears to be no particular theological or liturgical sequence to the icons in the upper two levels of the icon screen, although the topmost level depicts predominantly individual saints, while the middle level contains icons with multiple saints or festive days.

as president of the Eucharistic gathering. It is also symbolical of the collegiality of the body of bishops, chaired by the president of the local synod. The episcopal throne indicates the teaching authority of the bishop; the *synthronon* signifies the unity of love and faith that characterizes the Church.

The Icon of Panagia Faneromeni (7)

The icon of Panagia Faneromeni—literally, "the Mother of God, who appeared"—is a painted icon located in the left aisle of the church. This icon is honored for its miraculous properties. There are numerous styles of depicting the Mother of God. Like the mosaic of Panagia Pammakaristos (below), this particular icon depicts the Virgin Mother as "Hodigitria," which means "Directress" because she is pointing to the child Christ. The icon was transferred from Kizikos (present Kapıda□ in Turkey) and is overlaid with a gold and silver cover, or shirt. The figures of Mary and Christ are quite worn. The painting of the icon is estimated to date earlier than the Palaeologan renaissance of the fourteenth/fifteenth centuries.

The Icon of St. John the Forerunner (8)

The icon of St. John the Forerunner, or John the Baptist, is located in the right aisle of the church, on the right side of the iconostasis. It is traditionally believed that the original site of this icon was in the Church of Panagia Pammakaristos. This icon, too, is a mosaic and dates back to the eleventh century. Together with the icon of Panagia Pammakaristos, it predates the iconography found in Hagia Sophia and in the Monastery of Chora.

St. John is depicted pointing (to the Son of God) and bearing a scroll, which reads: "Behold, the lamb of God, who takes away the sin of the world."

The icon of Panagia Faneromeni (right).

The icon of St. John the Forerunner (far right).

The Icon of Panagia Pammakaristos (9)

The exquisite and rare mosaic icon of Panagia Pammakaristos (on the south wall to the right of the iconostasis), which depicts the Mother of God holding and pointing to the child Christ, was the patron icon of the ancient Byzantine church of Panagia Pammakaristos, which formerly served as Patriarchal church from 1486 to 1587. From there, the icon was transferred to each of the subsequent Patriarchal churches in Constantinople, including the present Church of St. George in the Phanar, where the icon has remained since the beginning of the seventeenth century. Its artistic style dates back to the late eleventh century, when the icon was created.

The icon of
Panagia
Pammakaristos.

The Column of Flagellation.

The Column of Christ's Flagellation (10)

Located in the southeast corner of the nave, this column is one of the most treasured and ancient relics of the Church of St. George. It is a portion of the column where our Lord was bound and whipped by Roman soldiers during His Passion and before His Crucifixion. Two other portions of this column are preserved in Jerusalem and in Rome. It is said to have been brought to Constantinople by St. Helen, the mother of Emperor Constantine, after she visited the Holy Land.

The Relics of St. Theophano (11)

Like icons, relics are a central aspect of Orthodox Christian worship. The theology of relics is grounded in the Orthodox doctrine of deification, or *theosis*, namely the sanctification of the entire human person—body and soul. They underline the fullness of the transfiguration of the material world by divine grace and serve as a reminder of the essential unity between the living Church and the Church triumphant. They are normally enshrined in elaborately crafted containers, or reliquaries, displayed for veneration and commemoration by the faithful.

The reliquaries of
St. Theophano, St. Euphemia,
and St. Solomone (left to right).

Evidence for the preservation and veneration of sacred relics dates back to at least the mid-second century. Popular veneration of relics further contributed to the unity of the Church during the Byzantine era.

The relics of three women saints of the Church are preserved intact in a row of reliquaries to the right of the Column of Flagellation. Those of St. Theophano are in the first reliquary.

St. Theophano the Empress came from a devout and noble family of Constantinople. She married Leo, an heir to the Byzantine Throne. Leo became known as Leo the Wise (886–911). Remarkably, while St. Theophano was born into an aristocratic house and married into the imperial palace, she always led an ascetic life. Hymnography recalls how she renounced earthly riches, leading instead a life of prayer and almsgiving. St. Theophano is commemorated on December 16.

St. Euphemia (icon in the Patriarchal House).

The Relics of St. Euphemia (12)

St. Euphemia, whose relics are in the middle reliquary, was born in Chalcedon (present-day Kadıköy), the daughter of devout parents, Philophron and Theodosiani. She was tortured during the persecutions of Emperors Diocletian and Maximian in the late third century. The Saint played a major role in inspiring the Fathers of the Fourth Ecumenical Council. During that council (451), St. Euphemia worked a miracle that determined the final doctrinal definition. The 630 Fathers, who gathered for this council in Chalcedon, were deliberating about the two natures of Christ. Eutyches and Dioscoros claimed that Christ possessed only a single nature. To test this teaching, the Holy Fathers inscribed the differing opinions on two separate decrees, which they placed inside the reliquary of St. Euphemia. When the reliquary was later opened, the decree of the heretics had fallen to the feet of the Saint, while the Orthodox doctrine rested in her hands. The Orthodox Church celebrates this miracle on July 11. The repose of St. Euphemia is commemorated on September 16.

According to her biography, the relics of St. Euphemia adorned many churches of Constantinople prior to its conquest in the fifteenth century. Thereafter, the relics were successively relocated to each of the Patriarchal churches. The icon of St. Euphemia records scenes from the life, martyrdom, and miraculous interventions of the Saint.

The Relics of St. Solomone (13)

St. Solomone, whose relics lie in the last reliquary on the right, was of Jewish ancestry, being the mother of the seven Maccabees—Abheim, Antonios, Gourias, f numerous Christian martyrs, who suffered torture at the hands of the State in the name of Christ. St. Solomone is commemorated on August 1.

Historians have suggested that the relics do not in fact belong to Solomone, since she was burned to death, being thrown into a fire with the Seven Maccabees. The relics probably belong to Mary Salome, one of the women who stood at the foot of the crucified Christ and one of the Myrrh-Bearing Women.

The Relics of St. Gregory the Theologian and St. John Chrysostom (14)

One of the most important Church Fathers, St. Gregory the Theologian (329–390) delivered five *Theological Orations* on the Holy Trinity and prepared the way for the triumph of orthodoxy during the Second Ecumenical Council (381), which completed the Symbol of Faith, also known as the [Nicean-Constantinopolitan] Creed. Regarded as the greatest of preachers, St. John Chrysostom (c.347–407) is one of the most beloved Church Fathers in both East and West. His sermons *On the Priesthood* remain formative reading on the ministry.

The relics of these two saints were taken to Rome after the Fourth Crusade in 1204, where they remained for 800 years. In November 2004, the sacred relics of the two renowned Archbishops of Constantinople were solemnly restored to the Ecumenical Patriarchate **(see page 56)**. They are now treasured in hand-carved marble reliquaries at the mid-point of the north wall of the nave of the Church of St. George.

The reliquaries of St. Gregory the Theologian (left)
and St. John Chrysostom (right).

The Buildings of the Ecumenical Patriarchate

The Constantiniana and the Evgenidio

Except for a small portion of the Patriarchal library, all of the buildings at the Phanar have been reconstructed in the last two centuries. The buildings situated on the western side of the Ecumenical Patriarchate are divided into two groups. The first group was constructed by Patriarch Constantine V toward the end of the nineteenth century. This group of buildings is called the "Constantiniana." It is linked to the second group by an iron bridge.

The second group of buildings was constructed as a Patriarchal residence by Patriarch Joachim III at the turn of the twentieth century. This group is called the "Evgenidio" because the project was sponsored by a banker, Efstathios Evgenidis. The two buildings of this group housed the offices of the Ecumenical Patriarchate from the time of Patriarch Benjamin (1936–1946) until recently.

A small, private chapel exists near the personal quarters of the Patriarch on the third floor of the "Evgenidio" building in the Ecumenical Patriarchate. It is dedicated to St. Andrew, the first-called of the Apostles and founder of the Church of Constantinople. The furnishings for this chapel were provided during the second tenure of Patriarch Joachim (1901–1912) by the generous gifts of Efstathios Evgenidis.

This chapel is used for special services, as foreseen by the Patriarchal protocol, as well as for daily personal prayer, particularly evening prayers, by the Patriarch.

The Patriarchal House

The most important buildings of the Ecumenical Patriarchate in the Phanar consisted of a group of four edifices, which were destroyed by fire in 1941. The fire, caused by a faulty electrical circuit, deprived the Ecumenical Patriarchate for over forty-six years of vital space, which housed the main offices. This central group of edifices consisted of a four-storey building constructed by Patriarch Germanos IV (1842–1845) and later renovated by Patriarch Joachim. The building contained a ground floor, a mezzanine floor,

The Patriarchal House, completely rebuilt between 1985 and 1987.

two floors of office space, an adjoining building, as well as two buildings for clergy and known as "Papadika."

In response to successive applications of the Ecumenical Patriarchate, the Turkish government granted permission for the reconstruction of the buildings destroyed by fire. This reconstruction occurred between 1985 and 1987, during the tenure of Patriarch Demetrios (1972–1991), largely through the generosity of Mr. Panagiotis Angelopoulos, who was subsequently awarded the title of Archon Megas Logothetis and Grand Benefactor of the Holy Mother Church of Christ. In this way, Mr. Angelopoulos rightfully joined the ranks of the other Grand Benefactors of the Church, Skylitsis, Mavrokordatos and Evgenidis, while the Ecumenical Patriarchate regained its proper glory.

Mr. Panagiotis Angelopoulos, whose generosity allowed for the reconstruction of the Patriarchal House, as well as the renovation of the Church of St. George.

The building was originally constructed in the eighteenth century in typical Turkish architectural style of the time. The restoration respected the original design, with modifications permitted only to the interior of the building, which was officially opened in December of 1989.

The main entrance to the Patriarchal House boasts three contemporary, yet creative mosaic panels. The first depicts the enthroned Christ holding the Book of Gospels and blessing those who enter. To his right, on a second panel, stands St. Andrew, "first-called of the Apostles" and founder of the Church of Constantinople; St. Andrew is portrayed handing the Gospel to his successor, St. Stachys, first bishop of the city of Byzantium. A third panel shows Sultan Mehmet II in his encounter with Gennadios Scholarios, first Ecumenical Patriarch after the Fall of Constantinople in 1453; Mehmet the Conqueror is offering a pastoral staff and a *ferman* (imperial edict) to the Patriarch, transferring privileges to the leader of the Orthodox Christians.

The new complex of buildings houses the various offices of the Ecumenical Patriarchate. The main floor contains the formal entrance and comprises the offices of the Patriarchal assistants and clergy, certain meeting rooms, and a dining hall for lay employees of the Ecumenical Patriarchate. The first (or mezzanine) floor contains the offices of the Grand Archdeaconry as well as a dining hall for the clergy and lay members, together with official guests, of the Patriarchal Court. The second floor consists of a reception room for various functions, called the Hall of the Virgin Mother,[10] a sitting room for bishops, known as the Room of Hierarchs, as well as the offices of the Chief Secretariat of the Holy Synod. The third and top floor houses the office of the Patriarch and the Private Patriarchal Office, the formal reception hall of the Ecumenical Patriarch, called the Hall of the Throne, the Hall of the Patriarchs with portraits of former Patriarchs, the Holy Synod Room, as well as the Patriarchal dining room.

The main entrance to the Patriarchal House (left) and the mosaic icon of the enthroned Christ at the top of the stairway (opposite page).

A second group of central buildings houses the Grand Chancellery, whose main office is situated on the third floor of the new complex, as well as three floors containing the living quarters of the Patriarchal Court, several guest rooms for visitors, and two apartments for visiting hierarchs.

---

[10] Named after a fourteenth-century icon of the Theotokos Hodigitria, or "Directress."

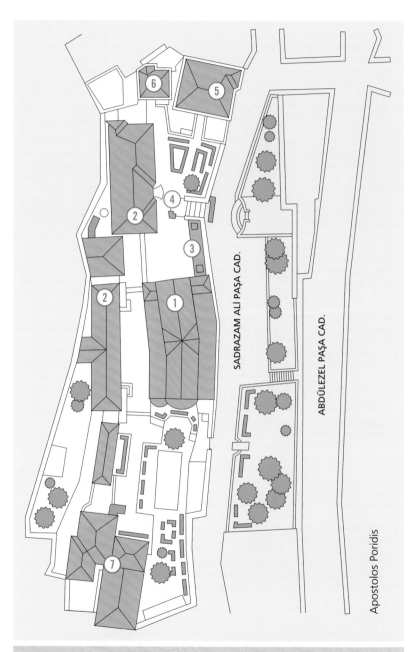

Plan of the Ecumenical Patriarchate
1. Church of St. George
2. Patriarchal House
3. Pavilion of the Holy Myron
4. Gate of Patriarch Gregory V
5. Evgenidio
6. Constantiniana
7. Tower and Adjoining Edifices (including the Patriarchal Library)

The Hall of the Throne, the official reception room of the Ecumenical Patriarch.

In addition to the expenses for the buildings mentioned above, the Grand Benefactor, Mr. Angelopoulos, sponsored the renovation of both the interior and the exterior of the Patriarchal Church of St. George, the complete furnishings in the buildings which formerly housed the Patriarchal offices, and a well that is situated in the courtyard of the Ecumenical Patriarchate.

The Gate of Patriarch Gregory V

Facing the Patriarchal House is the Gate of Patriarch Gregory V, who was martyred on Easter Sunday, 1821 (April 10), together with other members of the Holy Synod, only weeks prior to the declaration of the Greek War of Independence. Accused of conspiring with Greek revolutionists, Patriarch Gregory was hanged from this gate, which has remained closed out of reverent memorial to the hierarch, whose remains are preserved to this day in the cathedral of Athens, Greece.

It is also said that, during that period, the icon screen in the Patriarchal church was painted black as a sign of mourning. It was only recently restored to its former beauty, with the addition of gilding in 1994.

The Pavilion of the Holy Myron

A wooden, decorated pavilion is located in the courtyard. This is the site where the Holy Myrrh, or Myron, is prepared in special boilers during the days of Holy Week. When the amount of Holy Myron decreases and necessitates renewal, it is prepared in a series of formal rituals, commencing on Palm Sunday and culminating on Holy Thursday with a liturgical procession of all the Hierarchs of the Ecumenical Throne.

According to ancient and sacred tradition, Holy Myrrh is officially and solemnly consecrated by the Ecumenical Patriarch, whereupon it is distributed to Churches throughout the world as a profound sign of common faith and faith. The same Myrrh is used during the Sacrament of Holy Chrismation.

The present Patriarch has consecrated Holy Myrrh on two occasions, in Holy Week of 1992 and of 2003.

The Tower and Adjoining Edifices (including the Patriarchal Library)

Three buildings are located on the eastern side, behind the Church of St. George. Among them, the Tower or "the house built with stone, as it was named by Athanasios Ypsilantis." This eighteenth-century post-Byzantine edifice is characterized by its remarkable architecture and design. The first floor stores the Holy Myrrh and is known as the "Myrrhophylakion." The significance of the Holy Myrrh is described below. The second floor houses the archives and is known as the "Archiophylakion." The third floor contains the treasury (called the "Skevophylakion" or "Thesaurophylakion") and the sacristy (or "Kemeliophylakion") of the Ecumenical Patriarchate.

The wooden conference building of the Mixed Ecclesiastical Council adjoins the Tower. This edifice was constructed during the first tenure of Patriarch Joachim at the end of the nineteenth century. The first floor houses the office of the archivists and librarians of the Ecumenical Patriarchate. The second floor houses additional offices of these departments.

A third, stone building also adjoins the Tower. The first floor of this edifice was used for the Patriarchal printing offices, which operated from the seventeenth century until 1964. The second floor contains the treasures of the Patriarchal library, which was recently refurbished through the generosity of Mr. Theodore Papalexopoulos, Archon Maistor of the Great Church of Christ.

The Holy Synod Room
in the Patriarchal House.

The Return of the Relics of St. Gregory the Theologian and St. John Chrysostom

Historical Background

In November 2004, the sacred relics of two renowned Archbishops of Constantinople were solemnly restored to the Ecumenical Patriarchate, St. Gregory the Theologian (329–390) and St. John Chrysostom (c. 347–407). His All Holiness Ecumenical Patriarch Bartholomew I presided over a service of thanksgiving for their return and reception during the Thronal Feast of St. Andrew "the first-called of the Apostles." This historic occasion was the celebration and conclusion of a series of painful as well as joyful events.

The two saints served as Archbishops of Constantinople during the late fourth and early fifth centuries, a creative period for Christian theology and liturgy. St. Gregory was regarded as the theologian *par excellence*, delivering five extraordinary *Theological Orations* on the Holy Trinity and preparing the way for the triumph of orthodoxy during the Second Ecumenical Council (381), which completed the Symbol of Faith, also known as the [Nicean-Constantinopolitan] Creed. St. John is widely recognized as the greatest of preachers and one of the most popular of the Greek Church Fathers in both East and West; his remarkable sermons *On the Priesthood* remain formative reading on the ministry.

The relics of these Archbishops were formerly treasured in the Church of the Holy Apostles in Constantinople, where they lay side-by-side from the tenth century. St. Gregory was originally buried in Cappadocia, where he retired around 381; his relics were transferred to Constantinople in the tenth century by the Emperor Constantine Porphyrogenitus VII. St. John was originally buried in Koukousos of Asia Minor, where he died while in exile; his relics were returned to Constantinople in 438 by the Emperor Theodosius II.

The relics of the two saints were taken to Rome after the Fourth Crusade in 1204, which left a deep and lasting wound in the memory of the Orthodox Church. St. John Chrysostom's relics were placed in the medieval Church of St. Peter's at the Vatican, while St. Gregory the Theologian's were kept in the convent of St. Maria in Campo Santo.

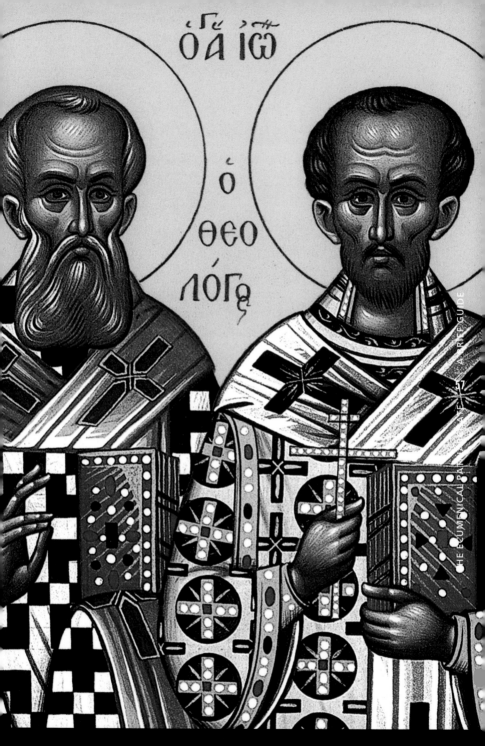

St. Gregory the Theologian (left) and
St. John Chrysostom (right).

Ecumenical Patriarch Bartholomew I and Pope
John Paul II at St. Peter's Basilica in Rome
(27 November 2004).

In 1580, with the construction of St. Peter's new basilica in the sixteenth century, Pope Gregory XIII transferred the relics of St. Gregory to a side altar, which came to be known as the Capella Gregoriana, in the nave of St. Peter's. In 1626, the relics of St. John were transferred to another altar in the nave, known as the Choir Chapel.[11]

The relics of the two Patriarchs of Constantinople remained in Rome for 800 years and in the new basilica of St. Peter's for 400 years.

Recent Events

In the early 1960s, in an act of fraternal fellowship, Pope Paul VI returned the sacred relics of certain saints belonging to the Orthodox Church, including those of St. Andrew (formerly preserved in the Amalfi, Italy) to Patras and St. Mark (formerly preserved in Venice, Italy) to the Coptic Church. The mid-1960s and 1970s also witnessed the extraordinary vision of Ecumenical Patriarch Athenagoras, who embarked on a "dialogue of love" with the Roman Catholic Church. In 1980, the "dialogue of truth" marked the commencement of the theological discussions between the two Churches.

---

[11] Information regarding manuscript evidence and medieval diagrams of these translations may be found in L. Rice, *Altars and Altarpieces of New St. Peter's*, Cambridge University Press, 1997. Details about the return of the relics were graciously provided by Dr. George Demacopoulos of Fordham University.

In June 2004, the Ecumenical Patriarch attended the Patronal Feast of the Roman Catholic Church (June 29). While the invitation is extended each year and the Ecumenical Patriarch is represented annually, that year also marked the 40th anniversary since the inception of the "dialogue of love" established in Jerusalem in 1964 as well as the 800th anniversary since the Fourth Crusade. On this occasion, Pope John Paul II officially apologized for the tragic events of the Fourth Crusade.[12]

In response, Ecumenical Patriarch Bartholomew I observed that no material compensation was at that time appropriate, but the rightful return of the sacred relics of the two Archbishops of Constantinople would comprise a spiritual restoration of that Church's legacy. The return of their relics would be a tangible gesture of the acknowledgement of past errors, a moral restoration of the spiritual legacy of the East, and a significant step in the process of reconciliation.

Ecumenical Patriarch Bartholomew I and His Eminence Cardinal Walter Kaspar in the Patriarchal Cathedral of St. George during the service of Thanksgiving for the return of the relics of St. Gregory the Theologian and St. John Chrysostom to the Ecumenical Patriarchate (27 November 2004).

---

[12] In 2001, during an official visit to the Church of Greece, Pope John Paul II extended an apology for the past offenses perpetrated against the Orthodox Church by the Roman Catholic Church, including the sacking of Constantinople during the Fourth Crusade.

Ecumenical Patriarch Bartholomew I personally accompanied the relics of the great Hierarchs to Constantinople on 27 November 2004, following an official service and ceremonial procession at St. Peter's in Rome. In the Cathedral of St. George, the crystal cases containing the relics were placed on the solea, immediately before the Patriarchal Throne. In accordance with ancient practice and protocol, during a service of Thanksgiving in the presence of representatives from all Orthodox Churches as well as a formal delegation from the Vatican led by Cardinal Walter Kasper, the Ecumenical Patriarch symbolically deferred to the Saints by offering the Throne in honor of their preeminence, while he sat in the *parathronion* or side-throne.

The return of relics is more than a purely historical event of theological importance; traditionally, it is a liturgical feast of spiritual significance. The new *Feast of the Translation of the Relics of St. Gregory the Theologian and St. John Chrysostom*, to be commemorated henceforth on November 30th as the official date of their reinstallation, will coincide with the Thronal Feast of the Church of Constantinople, namely the Feast of St. Andrew "the first-called of the Apostles."

What had begun in June of 2004, with the formal request of the relics during the Patronal Feast and inside the Basilica of St. Peter, concluded in November of 2004, with the solemn return of the relics during the Thronal Feast of the Mother Church of Constantinople, whose patron Saint is Andrew, the brother of St. Peter.[13]

The crystal cases containing the relics of St. Gregory the Theologian and St. John Chrysostom.

---

[13] The Order of St. Andrew, Archons in America, was invited by His All Holiness Ecumenical Patriarch Bartholomew to participate in both events (at the Vatican as well as in Constantinople). The delegation was led by the Exarch of the Ecumenical Patriarchate in North America, His Eminence Archbishop Demetrios, and included, among others, the Commander of the Archons of the Ecumenical Patriarchate, Dr. Anthony J. Limberakis, and Fr. Alexander Karloutsos.

This, too, was a further sign of the significant step toward reconciliation that occurred through the return of the sacred relics. The event has been memorialized in the new hymns composed by Metropolitan Evangelos of Perge. The relics are now treasured in the Patriarchal Cathedral of St. George in the Phanar, located at the mid-point of the north wall of the nave.

Hymns for the Translation of the Relics

Behold, the mystic of God and preacher of dogmas, Gregory the mind and glory of theology, comes to comfort us with his Relics; for he was our fellow-citizen from the ages and spoke before this very throne, as a divine treasure.

The Church once more rejoices splendidly on the arrival of your sacred Relic to the City, which you worthily shepherded; and she glorifies the heavenly Giver, O Father John Chrysostom, crying aloud: Behold your throne, O holy one.

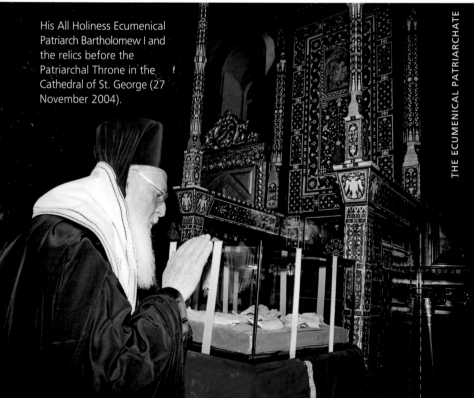

His All Holiness Ecumenical Patriarch Bartholomew I and the relics before the Patriarchal Throne in the Cathedral of St. George (27 November 2004).

Papal Visit to the Phanar

A Tradition of Love Continued

His All Holiness Ecumenical Patriarch Bartholomew received His Holiness Pope Benedict XVI on November 29 - 30, 2006 at the Ecumenical Patriarchate in Istanbul, Turkey. Pope Benedict's three-day visit to Istanbul came at the personal invitation of the Ecumenical Patriarch on the occasion of the feast day of Saint Andrew the Apostle, who traveled across Asia Minor and is

considered the founder of the Ecumenical Patriarchate. Both prelates are noted throughout the world as peacemakers and for their extraordinary efforts to create bridges of truth and love across religious, ethnic, environmental and political divides.

The visit of the Pope came toward the beginning of his Papal ministry and marked the revival of the theological dialogue between the two Churches, just as the visit of his predecessor, John Paul II, followed closely after his election to Pope and announced the beginning of the same dialogue, known as the Dialogue of Truth. Moreover, the visit by Pope Benedict was the first official visit of the Primate of the Roman Catholic Church to Istanbul in the past 27 years. The previous visit was in 1979 when Ecumenical Patriarch Dimitrios welcomed Pope John Paul II. The visit also constituted a historical continuity of previous meetings of Ecumenical Patriarch Athenagoras and Pope Paul VI, who proclaimed the lifting of the anathemas (excommunications), which accompanied the great Schism of the Church and divided Christianity in 1054.

Ecumenical Patriarch
Bartholomew I and Pope
Benedict XVI enter the
Patriarchal Cathedral
of St. George
(29 November 2006).

Ecumenical Patriarch Bartholomew I greets Pope Benedict XVI. The Pope's visit came at the invitation of the Ecumenical Patriarch on the occasion of the feast day of St. Andrew.

Pope Benedict XVI arrived in Istanbul, on Wednesday afternoon, November 29, in order to attend a Doxology of Peace at the Patriarchal Cathedral of St. George. The prayer service included a mutual veneration of the Holy Relics of Saint Gregory the Theologian and Saint John Chrysostom, the sacred Predecessors of the Ecumenical Patriarch, and was followed by a private meeting between the two Church leaders.

On Thursday morning, November 30, Benedict XVI attended the Divine Liturgy at St. George Cathedral, where both prelates delivered official addresses, exchanged the Kiss of Peace, and jointly blessed the faithful present. After the Divine Liturgy, a Common Declaration of ecumenical solidarity was read and signed.

After receiving the Ecumenical Patriarch at the Roman Catholic Church of the Holy Spirit and celebrating the Papal Holy Mass, Pope Benedict departed for Vatican City on Friday, December 1, 2006.

Common Declaration by Pope Benedict and Ecumenical Patriarch Bartholomew
"This is the day that the Lord has made, let us rejoice and be glad in it!" (*Ps* 117:24)

This fraternal encounter which brings us together, Pope Benedict XVI of Rome and Ecumenical Patriarch Bartholomew I, is God's work, and in a certain sense his gift. We give thanks to the Author of all that is good, who allows us once again, in prayer and in dialogue, to express the joy we feel as brothers and to renew our commitment to move towards full communion. This commitment comes from the Lord's will and from our responsibility as Pastors in the Church of Christ. May our meeting be a sign and an encouragement to us to share the same sentiments and the same attitudes encouragement to us to share the same sentiments and the same attitudes of fraternity, cooperation and communion in charity and truth. The Holy Spirit will help us to prepare the great day of the re-establishment of full unity, whenever and however God wills it. Then we shall truly be able to rejoice and be glad.

1. We have recalled with thankfulness the meetings of our venerable predecessors, blessed by the Lord, who showed the world the urgent need for unity and traced sure paths for attaining it, through dialogue, prayer and the daily life of the Church. Pope Paul VI and Patriarch Athenagoras I went as pilgrims to Jerusalem, to the very place where Jesus Christ died and rose again for the salvation of the world, and they also met again, here in the Phanar and in Rome. They left us a common declaration which retains all its value; it emphasizes that true dialogue in charity must sustain and inspire all relations between individuals and between Churches, that it "'must be rooted in a total fidelity to the one Lord Jesus Christ and in mutual respect for their own traditions" (*Tomos Agapis*, 195). Nor have we forgotten the reciprocal visits of His Holiness Pope John Paul II and His Holiness Dimitrios I. It was during the visit of Pope John Paul II, his first ecumenical visit, that the creation of the Mixed Commission for theological dialogue between the Roman Catholic Church and the Orthodox Church was announced. This has brought together our Churches in the declared aim of re-establishing full communion.

As far as relations between the Church of Rome and the Church of Constantinople are concerned, we cannot fail to recall the solemn ecclesial act effacing the memory of the ancient anathemas which for centuries had a negative effect on our Churches. We have not yet drawn from this act

Ecumenical Patriarch Bartholomew I and Pope Benedict XVI in front of the iconostasis in the Cathedral of St. George.

all the positive consequences which can flow from it in our progress towards full unity, to which the mixed Commission is called to make an important contribution. We exhort our faithful to take an active part in this process, through prayer and through significant gestures.

2. At the time of the plenary session of the mixed Commission for theological dialogue, which was recently held in Belgrade through the generous hospitality of the Serbian Orthodox Church, we expressed our profound joy at the resumption of the theological dialogue. This had been interrupted for several years because of various difficulties, but now the Commission was able to work afresh in a spirit of friendship and cooperation. In treating the topic "'Conciliarity and Authority in the Church" at local, regional and universal levels, the Commission undertook a phase of study on the ecclesiological and canonical consequences of the sacramental nature of the Church. This will permit us to address some of the principal questions that are still unresolved. We are committed to offer unceasing support, as in the past, to the work entrusted to this Commission and we accompany its members with our prayers.

3. As Pastors, we have first of all reflected on the mission to proclaim the Gospel in today's world. This mission, "'Go, make disciples of all nations" (*Mt* 28:19), is today more timely and necessary than ever, even in traditionally Christian countries. Moreover, we cannot ignore the increase of secularization, relativism, even nihilism, especially in the Western world. All this calls for a renewed and powerful proclamation of the Gospel, adapted to the cultures of our time. Our traditions represent for us a patrimony which must be continually shared, proposed, and interpreted anew. This is why we must strengthen our cooperation and our common witness before the world.

4. We have viewed positively the process that has led to the formation of the European Union. Those engaged in this great project should not fail to take into consideration all aspects affecting the inalienable rights of the human person, especially religious freedom, a witness and guarantor of respect for all other freedoms. In every step towards unification, minorities must be protected, with their cultural traditions and the distinguishing features of their religion. In Europe, while remaining open to other religions and to their cultural contributions, we must unite our efforts to preserve Christian roots, traditions and values, to ensure respect for history, and thus to contribute to the European culture of the future and to the quality of human relations at every level. In this context, how could we not evoke the very ancient witnesses and the illustrious Christian heritage of the land in which our meeting is taking place, beginning with what the *Acts of the Apostles* tells us concerning the figure of Saint Paul, Apostle of the Gentiles? In this land, the Gospel message and the ancient cultural tradition met. This link, which has contributed so much to the Christian heritage that we share, remains timely and will bear more fruit in the future for evangelization and for our unity.

5. Our concern extends to those parts of today's world where Christians live and to the difficulties they have to face, particularly poverty, wars and terrorism, but equally to various forms of exploitation of the poor, of migrants, women and children. We are called to work together to promote respect for the rights of every human being, created in the image and likeness of God, and to foster economic, social and cultural development. Our theological and ethical traditions can offer a solid basis for a united approach in preaching and action. Above all, we wish to affirm that killing innocent people in God's name is an offence against him and against human dignity. We must all commit ourselves to the renewed service of humanity and the defense of human life, every human life.

The leaders of the Orthodox and Roman Catholic Churches greeting the faithful after the celebration the Divine Liturgy on the Feast of St. Andrew (30 November 2006).

We take profoundly to heart the cause of peace in the Middle East, where our Lord lived, suffered, died and rose again, and where a great multitude of our Christian brethren have lived for centuries. We fervently hope that peace will be re-established in that region, that respectful coexistence will be strengthened between the different peoples that live there, between the Churches and between the different religions found there. To this end, we encourage the establishment of closer relationships between Christians, and of an authentic and honest interreligious dialogue, with a view to combating every form of violence and discrimination.

6. At present, in the face of the great threats to the natural environment, we want to express our concern at the negative consequences for humanity and for the whole of creation which can result from economic and technological progress that does not know its limits. As religious leaders, we consider it one of our duties to encourage and to support all efforts made to protect God's creation, and to bequeath to future generations a world in which they will be able to live.

7. Finally, our thoughts turn towards all of you, the faithful of our two Churches throughout the world, Bishops, priests, deacons, men and women religious, lay men and women engaged in ecclesial service, and all the baptized. In Christ we greet other Christians, assuring them of our prayers and our openness to dialogue and cooperation. In the words of the Apostle of the Gentiles, we greet all of you: "'Grace to you and peace from God our Father and the Lord Jesus Christ" (*2 Cor* 1:2).

At the Phanar, 30 November 2006

Synaxis of the Heads of Orthodox Churches

A Powerful Symbol of Unity

The unity of the Church is a fragile gift, entrusted to us by God and embodied in the meeting of minds of Church leaders coming together in council to deliberate and in communion through liturgy. His All Holiness Ecumenical Patriarch Bartholomew recognizes the value and fragility alike of this divine gift, working from his position as "first among equals" to facilitate common celebration and common action. Admittedly, his delicate work of balance and coordination is not always appreciated. Nevertheless, on October 10, 2008, Orthodox Christians throughout the world witnessed the Heads of all Orthodox Churches assembling for the fifth time under the tenure of this Ecumenical Patriarch, who first established the hitherto unprecedented institution of the Synaxis. The latest Synaxis was held in Constantinople from October 10 to 12, 2008, with Patriarchs and Archbishops meeting together, producing a Common Declaration, and celebrating the Divine Liturgy in the Patriarchal Church of St. George.

The Synaxis was chaired by the Ecumenical Patriarch, while the Hierarchs in attendance included the Patriarchs of Alexandria, Antioch, Jerusalem, and Moscow, as well as senior representatives from the Patriarchates of Serbia, Romania, Bulgaria and Georgia. Also present were the Archbishops of Cyprus and Athens, senior representatives from the Church of Poland, the Archbishops of Albania and Prague, as well as of Finland and Estonia.

In his opening address, the Ecumenical Patriarch offered several recommendations for common action among the Hierarchs [see excerpts from his address below], most notably including the advancement of preparations for the Great Council of the Orthodox Church and the activation of the 1993 agreement of the Inter-Orthodox Consultation of the Holy and Great Council in order to resolve issues related to the Orthodox Diaspora.

On Sunday morning, the Divine Liturgy was celebrated by all the above Hierarchs, together with the Metropolitans of Chalcedon and Kiev, as well as Archbishop Demetrios of America and Metropolitan Kornilios of Tallinn of the Moscow Patriarchate. The Divine Liturgy was followed by a Trisagion Service held at Baloukli Monastery in memory of all Ecumenical Patriarchs (who are buried there) and other Heads of Orthodox Churches who have passed away.

The Synaxis meeting and celebration were powerful and visible symbols of unity for Orthodox leaders and their faithful all over the world.

From the Address by His All Holiness Ecumenical Patriarch Bartholomew:

From the moment that, by God's mercy, we assumed the reins of this First Throne among Churches, we have regarded it as our sacred obligation and duty to strengthen the bonds of love and unity of all those entrusted with the leadership of the local Orthodox Churches. Thus, in response also to the desire of other brothers serving as Heads, we took the initiative of convoking several occasions for Synaxis: first, in this City on the Sunday of Orthodoxy in 1992; then, on the sacred island of Patmos in 1995; and thereafter, we had the blessing of experiencing similar encounters and concelebrations in Jerusalem and the Phanar on the occasion of the beginning and end of the year 2000 as we entered this third millennium of the Lord's era.

Of course, these occasions for Synaxis do not comprise an "'institution" by canonical standards. As known, the sacred Canons of our Church assign the supreme responsibility and authority for decisions on ecclesiastical matters to the Synodical system, wherein all hierarchs in active ministry participate either in rotation or in plenary. This canonical establishment is by no means substituted by the Synaxis of the Heads of Churches. Nevertheless, from time to time, such a Synaxis is deemed necessary and beneficial, especially in times like ours, when the personal encounter and conversation among responsible leaders in all public domains of human life is rendered increasingly accessible and essential. Therefore, the benefit gained from a personal encounter of the Heads of the Orthodox Churches can, with God's grace, only prove immense. ...

Church unity is not merely an internal matter of the Church ... because Church unity is inextricably linked with the unity of all humanity. The Church does not exist for itself but for all humankind and, still more broadly, for the whole of creation. ...

Celebration of the Divine Liturgy during the Synaxis.

Ecumenical Patriarch Bartholomew I chairs the Synaxis of the Heads of the Orthodox Churches (10–12 October 2008).

His All Holiness Ecumenical Patriarch
Bartholomew I leads a con-celebration
of the Divine Liturgy during the Synaxis.

Of course, the response commonly proffered to this question is that, despite administrational division, Orthodoxy remains united in faith, the Sacraments, etc. But is this sufficient? When before non-Orthodox we sometimes appear divided in theological dialogues and elsewhere; when we are unable to proceed to the realization of the long-heralded Holy and Great Council of the Orthodox Church; when we lack a unified voice on contemporary issues and, instead, convoke bilateral dialogues with non-Orthodox on these issues; when we fail to constitute a single Orthodox Church in the so-called Diaspora in accordance with the ecclesiological and canonical principles of our Church; how can we avoid the image of division in Orthodoxy, especially on the basis of non-theological, secular criteria?

We need, then, greater unity in order to appear to those outside not as a federation of Churches but as one unified Church. Through the centuries, and especially after the Schism, when the Church of Rome ceased to be in communion with the Orthodox, this Throne was called – according to canonical order – to serve the unity of the Orthodox Church as its First Throne. And it fulfilled this responsibility through the ages by convoking an entire series of Panorthodox Councils on crucial ecclesiastical matters, always prepared, whenever duly approached, to render its assistance and support to troubled Orthodox Churches. In this way, a canonical order was created and, accordingly, the coordinating role of this Patriarchate guaranteed the unity of the Orthodox Church, without in the least damaging or diminishing the independence of the local autocephalous Churches by any interference in their internal affairs. This, in any case, is the healthy significance of the institution of autocephaly: while it assures the self-governance of each Church with regard to its internal life and organization, on matters affecting the entire Orthodox Church and its relations with those outside, each autocephalous Church does not act alone but in coordination with the rest of the Orthodox Churches. If this coordination either disappears or diminishes, then autocephaly becomes "'autocephalism" (or radical independence), namely a factor of division rather than unity for the Orthodox Church.

Therefore, dearly beloved brothers in the Lord, we are called to contribute in every possible way to the unity of the Orthodox Church, transcending every temptation of regionalism or nationalism so that we may act as a unified Church, as one canonically structured body. We do not, as during

Byzantine times, have at our disposal a state factor that guaranteed – and sometimes even imposed – our unity. Nor does our ecclesiology permit any centralized authority that is able to impose unity from above. Our unity depends on our conscience. The sense of need and duty that we constitute a single canonical structure and body, one Church, is sufficient to guarantee our unity, without any external intervention.

Proposals by His All Holiness Ecumenical Patriarch Bartholomew to the Heads of the Orthodox Churches:

a) To advance the preparations for the Holy and Great Council of the Orthodox Church, already commenced through Panorthodox Pre-Conciliar Consultations.

b) To activate the 1993 agreement of the Inter-Orthodox Consultation of the Holy and Great Council in order to resolve the pending matter of the Orthodox Diaspora.

c) To strengthen by means of further theological support the decisions taken on a Panorthodox level regarding participation of the Orthodox Church in theological dialogues with non-Orthodox.

d) To proclaim once again the vivid interest of the entire Orthodox Church for the crucial and urgent matter of protecting the natural environment, supporting on a Panorthodox level the relative initiative of the Ecumenical Patriarchate.

e) To establish an Inter-Orthodox Committee for the study of matters arising today in the field of bioethics, on which the world justifiably also awaits the Orthodox position.

The Year of St. Paul

An Academic and Pastoral Symposium

In his 2007 Christmas Encyclical, His All Holiness Ecumenical Patriarch Bartholomew proclaimed 2008 as a Year dedicated to St. Paul "in remembrance of his words and works, as well as in celebration of two millennia since his birth." The year 8AD is conventionally estimated by scholars to be around the year of St. Paul's birth.

Two extraordinary and historical events were planned for the celebration: first, the Synaxis of the Heads of the Orthodox Churches, which met in Constantinople from October 10th to 12th, 2008, at the invitation of the Ecumenical Patriarch; and, second, again at the invitation of the Ecumenical Patriarch, a Pauline Symposium that traveled from October 11th to 16th, 2008, through cities of Turkey and Greece where St. Paul preached during his missionary journeys.

Specifically organized within the context of the Year of St. Paul and within the ecclesiastical framework of – and as a scholarly offering to – the Synaxis, the Symposium drew recognized scholars from diverse Christian communions and numerous countries for a Symposium, officially opening in Constantinople (Istanbul) and proceeding through the cities of Smyrna, Ephesus, Perge and Antalya (in Asia Minor), as well as Lindos (Rhodes) and Kaloi Limenes (Crete), where it officially concluded. While the formal language of the Symposium was English, there was simultaneous Greek and Russian translation to cater to the Patriarchs and Hierarchs from all Orthodox Churches throughout the world. His Eminence Archbishop Demetrios of America was chairman of the academic committee, presiding over the sessions throughout the Symposium, while His Eminence Metropolitan Gennadios of Sassima was chairman of the organizing committee.

The Ecumenical Patriarch led the Symposium, accompanied by the Patriarch of Alexandria, the Archbishop of Cyprus, the Archbishop of Athens, the Archbishop of Albania, and the Archbishop of Prague, as well as representatives from every Autocephalous and Autonomous Church, including the Patriarchates of Antioch, Jerusalem, Moscow, Serbia, Romania, Bulgaria, and Georgia, as well as the Churches of Poland, Finland and Estonia. The

Ecumenical Patriarch Bartholomew I and Heads of the Orthodox Churches in Rhodes, Greece, during the Pauline Symposium (11–16 October 2008).

Roman Catholic Church was represented throughout by personal delegates of Pope Benedict XVI.

Speakers included His Eminence Archbishop Demetrios (*St. Paul as Apostle, Pastor and Theologian*), Bishop Tom Wright of Durham (*Eschatology in St. Paul*), Prof. Petros Vasileiadis (*Freedom in St. Paul*), Prof. Christos Voulgaris (*The Cosmic Dimensions of Christ's Redemption*), Prof. Helmut Koester (*The Charismata of the Spirit*), Prof. Karl Donfried (*The Life "in Christ"*), Prof. Brian Daley (*Paul in the Fathers of the Church*), Prof. Ioannis Karavidopoulos (*Paul as Theological Bridge between East and West*), V. Rev. Dr. Jacques Khalil (*The Bishop in Paul's Pastoral Letters*), and Prof. Turid Karlsen Seim (*Race and Gender in Paul*). Session moderators included His Eminence Metropolitan Gennadios of Sassima, Prof. Christos Oikonomou, Prof. John Fotopoulos, and Rev. Dr. John Chryssavgis (who also served as secretary of the academic committee).

The 90 participants of the Symposium enjoyed the generous hospitality of the Ecumenical Patriarchate as they traveled through Turkey and Greece. In Ephesus and Perge, they received a guided tour by Prof. Helmut Koester of Harvard University (also a Symposium speaker), while the sessions in Rhodes were held at the very site of several historical Panorthodox consultations as well as the opening of the Official Theological Dialogue between the Roman Catholic and Orthodox Churches. Nothing could quite

The Pauline Symposium was attended by 90 participants, who traveled to various holy sites associated with St. Paul in Turkey and Greece, such as Ephesus.

prepare the Patriarchs, hierarchs and delegates as they were welcomed in Crete by numerous faithful, who spontaneously lined the streets for miles with rose petals, palm leaves and incense. It is difficult to imagine the warm hospitality extended to the Patriarchs. Yet, Crete had never before witnessed as auspicious an hierarchical gathering as this.

The Symposium proceedings were videotaped by the Greek Orthodox Archdiocese of America and, together with a formal publication of the major addresses, will soon be available to parishes and the general public.

From the Opening Address by His All Holiness Ecumenical Patriarch Bartholomew:

We offer praise and glory to the Trinitarian God for the spiritual banquet that lies before us and that we are blessed officially to open this afternoon following the successful conclusion this morning of an historical Synaxis, which has gathered the Heads of Autocephalous and Autonomous Orthodox Churches throughout the world in a powerful and symbolical affirmation of our unity in faith and commitment of purpose as Hierarchs entrusted with leadership of our Churches in the contemporary world. As we assembled we recognize that, truly, "our ministry overflows with many thanksgivings to God." (2 Cor. 9.12) ...

While St. Paul was not the author of systematic treatises, it is generally acknowledged that there is hardly an area of Christian theology or Pneumatology, of Christology or ecclesiology, of anthropology or soteriology, indeed of ethics or ecology, for which St. Paul did not sow the seeds in his "bold" proclamation of the Gospel. ...

In order, then, to realize the all-embracing importance and impact of this great Apostle, we have chosen to follow in the footsteps of his missionary journeys through key cities of Asia Minor and Greece. Over the next week, we will quite literally be walking and conversing with St. Paul, discerning his traces and discussing his concepts. And so, in scholarly and spiritual fellowship, we shall travel together from this City to Smyrna (one of the cities along St. Paul's third missionary journey); to Ephesus (where St. Paul met "in the church in the house" of Prisca and Aquila, those "who risked their necks for his life" [cf. Rom. 16.3-5]; it is in Ephesus where Paul also preached that "gods made by human hands are no gods at all" [Acts 19.26]); and to Attaleia (the ancient Roman port where St. Paul preached the Gospel and then set sail to Antioch [cf. Acts 14.25]), as well as to Rhodes (where an entire bay is named after the great Apostle, who landed there toward the middle of the first century); and Crete (where Paul left Titus to serve as first bishop). We can only be in eternal awe of St. Paul's remarkable endurance and perilous travels. ...

St. Paul is justifiably considered the theologian of unity and of freedom alike. For, while he perceived the crucial distinction between unity and uniformity, he also professed the critical value of openness or freedom, affirming diversity and discerning the joy of Christ in "whatever is true, whatever is honorable, whatever is just, whatever is pure, whatever is pleasing, whatever is commendable, wherever there is excellence and anything worthy of praise." (Phil. 4.8) In its catholicity, the Orthodox Church is truly and profoundly "ecumenical." Nevertheless, this catholicity or ecumenicity is not "universal" – in the etymological sense of the word (from the Latin "tending toward oneness"), in the literal sense of drawing all things to unilateral homogeneity. This, as we underlined yesterday to our brother Bishops during the Hierarchal Synaxis, is the crucial basis of and essential criterion for Paul's passionate plea for Church unity "in the same mind and purpose." (1 Cor. 1.10) Nevertheless, at the same time, St. Paul prefers to emphasize "conformity" to the Body of Christ – "until Christ is formed in you" (Gal. 4.19) – rather than "uniformity" in accordance with certain ethical prescriptions. This is a unity that can only be realized in dialogue and collegiality, not in any universal imposition of opinion or doctrine.

Appendix I

The Immediate Jurisdiction of the Ecumenical Patriarchate

The Archdiocese of Constantinople
  District of Stavrodromion
  District of Tataoula
  District the Bosphorus
  District of Hypsomatheia
  District of Phanar

Sacred Metropolitanates in Turkey
  Metropolitanate of Chalcedon
  Metropolitanate of Derkon
  Metropolitanate of Imvros and Tenedos
  Metropolitanate of the Princes Islands

The Semi-Autonomous Archdiocese of Crete
  Metropolitanate of Gortini and Arcadia
  Metropolitanate of Rethimno and Aulopotamos
  Metropolitanate of Kidonia and Apokoronon
  Metropolitanate of Lambi, Sivrito, and Sfakia
  Metropolitanate of Ierapitni and Sitia
  Metropolitanate of Petra and Hersonissos
  Metropolitanate of Kissamos and Selinos
  Metropolitanate of Arkalohorio, Castellion, and Viannos

Five Metropolitanates of the Dodecanese Islands
  Metropolitanate of Rhodes
  Metropolitanate of Kos and Nisiros
  Metropolitanate of Leros, Kalimnos, and Astipalea
  Metropolitanate of Karpathos and Kassos
  Metropolitanate of Simi

The Archdiocese of America
  Direct Archdiocesan District (New York)
  Metropolitanate of Chicago
  Metropolitanate of San Francisco
  Metropolitanate of Pittsburg
  Metropolitanate of Boston
  Metropolitanate of Denver
  Metropolitanate of Atlanta
  Metropolitanate of Detroit
  Metropolitanate of New Jersey

The Archdiocese of Australia
The Archdiocese of Thyateira and Great Britain and Ireland
The Metropolitanate of France
The Metropolitanate of Germany
The Metropolitanate of Austria and Hungary
The Metropolitanate of Sweden and All Scandinavia (Norway, Denmark)
The Metropolitanate of Belgium (Holland and Luxemburg)
The Metropolitanate of New Zealand
The Metropolitanate of Switzerland
The Metropolitanate of Italy and Malta
The Metropolitanate of Toronto (Canada)
The Ukrainian Diocese of Canada
The Metropolitanate of Buenos Aires (Argentina, South America)
The Metropolitanate of Mexico (Central America)
The Metropolitanate of Hong Kong (India, Philippine Islands, Singapore, Indonesia)
The Metropolitanate of Spain and Portugal
The Metropolitanate of Korea (Exarchate of Japan)
The Patriarchal Exarchate of the Russian Orthodox Parishes in Western Europe (Paris)

Thirty-six Metropolitanates of the "New Lands" in Northern Greece and some of the Aegean Islands* also fall under the spiritual and canonical jurisdiction of the Ecumenical Patriarchate; however, their administration was entrusted to the Church of Greece on behalf of the Ecumenical Patriarchate in the year 1928.

---

* Including Alexandroupolis, Veroia (and Naoussa), Goumenissa (with Axioupolis and Polykastron), Grevena, Didymoteichon (and Orestias), Drama, Dryinoupolis (Pogoniani and Konitsa), Edessa (and Pella), Elasson, Eleftheroupolis, Zichna (and Nevrokopion), Thessaloniki, Ierissos (and Adramerion), Ioannina, Kassandra, Kastoria, Kitrous, Laggada, Lemnos, Maronia (and Komotini), Mithimni, Mytilini, Neapolis (and Stavroupolis), Nea Krini (and Kalamaria), Nikopolis (and Preveza), Xanthi, Paramythia (with Filiata and Giromerion), Polyani (and Kilkision), Samos (and Ikaria), Servia (and Kozani), Serres (and Nigriti), Siderokastron, Sissanion (and Siatista), Philippi (with Neapolis and Thassos), Florina (with Prespa and Eordaia), and Chios.

Patriarchal and Stavropegial Monasteries outside of Turkey

The Monastery of St. John the Evangelist and the Exarchate of Patmos, Greece
Mount Athos (the historic self-governing monastic community in Northern Greece, comprised of 20 large monasteries, their dependencies and approximately 2000 monks)
The Monastery of St. Anastasia Pharmakolitria, Halkidiki, Greece
The Monastery of Vlatadoes, Thessaloniki, Greece
The Monastery of St. John the Forerunner, Essex, Great Britain
The Monastery of the Entry of the Virgin Mary, Alabama, U.S.A.
The Monastery of St. Irene Chrysovalantou, New York, U.S.A.

Patriarchal Foundations outside of Turkey

Institute for Patristic Studies in Thessaloniki
Vice Chairman: Metropolitan Panteleimon of Tyroloi and Serention
Holy Monastery of Vlatadon, 64 Eptapyrgion Street, 54634 Thessaloniki, Greece, Tel. +30 2310 202 301; Fax: 200 637

Orthodox Center in Chambesy
Director: Metropolitan Jeremiah of Switzerland, 37 Chemin de Chambesy, CH-1292 Chambesy, Switzerland, Tel. +41 (0) 22 758 9860; Fax: 758 9861

Institution for Orthodox Missionary Work in the Far East
Chairman: Dr. Ioannis Lappas, Gounaropoulou 3, 157 71 Zographou, Attikis, Athens, Greece, Tel. +30 210 771 0732; Fax: 778 0541

Patriarch Athenagoras Orthodox Institute, Berkley, CA
Director: Dr. Anton Vrame, 2309 Hearst Avenue, Berkley, CA, 94709-1319, U.S.A., Tel. +1 510 649 3450; Fax: 841 6605
www.orthodoxinstitute.org; paoi@gtu.edu

Institute for Post-Graduate Studies of Orthodox Theology in Chambesy
37 Chemin de Chambesy, CH-1292 Chambesy, Switzerland, Tel. +41 22 758 9864; Fax: 758 9895, orthodoxinstitute@yahoo.com

Foundation for the Patronage of the Ecumenical Patriarchate in Athens
Chairman: His Grace Bishop Makarios of Knossos, Notara 131, 185 36 Piraeus, Greece, Tel. +30 210 429 4402; Fax: 429 4409

Patriarchal Organizations outside of Turkey

Permanent Representation Office at the World Council of Churches
Representative: Archimandrite Benedict Ioannou,
150 Route de Ferney, PO Box 2100, GH-1211 Geneve 2, Switzerland,
Tel. +41 (0) 22 791 6348; Fax: 791 6346; ecupatria@wcc-coe.org

Secretariat Committee for the Preparation of the Holy and
Great Synod of the Orthodox Church
Director: His Eminence Metropolitan Jeremiah of Switzerland,
37 Chemin de Chambesy, CH-1292 Chambesy, Switzerland,
Tel. +41 (0) 22 758 9860; Fax: 758 9861

The Order of the Holy and Great Church of Christ
"Panaghia Pammakaristos"
President: Mr. Ioannis Papamichalakis, Regillis 26, 106 74 Athens, Greece
Tel. +30 210 723 5735; Fax: 724 0000

Liaison Office of the Orthodox Church to the European Union
Director: His Eminence Metropolitan Emmanuel of France
Place de Jamblinne de Meux 40, 1030 Brussels, Belgium,
Tel. +32 2 734 8987; Fax: 734 9072; OEU@compuserve.com

Office of the Representative of the Ecumenical Patriarchate in Athens
Director: His Eminence Metropolitan John of Pergamon,
Neophytou Douka 9, 106 74 Athens, Greece,
Tel. +30 210 725 7862, Fax: 725 2540; oikpat@otenet.gr

Appendix II

Feast Days of the Ecumenical Patriarchate

After the central Feast of Pascha, or Easter, and the Sunday commemoration of the Resurrection, the Orthodox Church celebrates several feast days, including the Twelve Great Feasts recalling the saving events connected with Christ's life. Most of these feasts were established as early as from the fourth to the sixth centuries. Starting from September 1st that marks the beginning of the Christian ecclesiastical year, just as the Jewish year, they include: the Nativity of the Theotokos (September 8), the Exaltation of the Cross (September 14), the Entrance of the Theotokos into the Temple (November 21), the Nativity of our Lord, or Christmas (December 25), the Baptism of our Lord known as Epiphany, or Theophany (January 6), the Meeting of our Lord in the Temple (February 2), the Annunciation (March 25), Palm Sunday (one week prior to Easter; a moveable feast, depending on the annual date of Easter), the Ascension of our Lord (forty days after Easter), Pentecost (fifty days after Easter), the Transfiguration of our Lord (August 6), and the Dormition of the Theotokos (August 15).

In addition to these great feasts, the Orthodox Church commemorates numerous saintly lives and miraculous events throughout the year. In addition to the solemn commemoration of Saturdays and the festive celebration of Sundays, the Ecumenical Patriarchate also keeps certain of these holy days as administrative holidays. Major holidays at the Phanar include:

January 1	Feast of St. Basil the Great, Archbishop of Caesarea of Cappadocia
January 6	Feast of the Theophany, the Baptism of the Lord
January 30	Feast of the Three Hierarchs
March 25	Feast of the Annunciation
April 23	Feast of St. George the Trophy Bearer, feast day of the Patriarchal Church (This is a movable feast, dependant on the annual celebration of Easter. Other such holiday

feasts include Clean Monday, or the first day of Lent, Holy Thursday and Great Friday, as well as Monday of Bright Week and Monday of the Holy Spirit)

June 11	Feast of St. Bartholomew the Apostle, Name Day of Ecumenical Patriarch Bartholomew I
June 29	Feast of Sts. Peter and Paul
August 15	Dormition of the Theotokos
September 1	Opening of the ecclesiastical year, known as the Indiktos; Day of prayer for the protection of the natural environment
September 14	Elevation of the Holy Cross
November 21	Entrance of the Theotokos into the Temple
November 30	Thronal, or Patronal feast day: Commemoration of St. Andrew, the "first-called of the Apostles"
December 25	Feast of the Nativity of the Lord

Appendix III

Ecumenical Councils of the Orthodox Church

The "Great" or "Ecumenical" Councils, accepted by both East and West, and adopted by a large part of Christendom inasmuch as they defined and defended the fundamental doctrines of the Christian Church, were held either in or near the city of Constantinople.

I. Nicaea

325

Main Teaching: formulated the first part of the Symbol of Faith, known as the "Nicaean Creed," defining the divinity of the Son of God

II. Constantinople

381

Main Teaching: formulated the second part of the Symbol of Faith, defining the divinity of the Holy Spirit. The "Nicaean-Constantinopolitan Creed" remains unchanged in the Orthodox Church since the fourth century. It is recited at every baptism and repeated during each Divine Liturgy

III. Ephesus

431

Main Teaching: proclaimed Jesus Christ as the Incarnate Word of God and Mary as the Theotokos

IV. Chalcedon

451

Main Teaching: proclaimed Jesus Christ as fully divine and fully human, two natures in one person

V. Constantinople

553

Main Teaching: confirmed the doctrines of the Holy Trinity and the person of Jesus Christ

VI. Constantinople **680–681**
Main Teaching: affirmed the full humanity of Jesus Christ by insisting on the reality of His human will

Penthekti (or Quinisext) **692**
Main Teaching: completed the doctrinal teaching of the fifth and sixth Ecumenical Councils

VII. Nicaea **787**
Main Teaching: affirmed the use of icons as genuine expressions of the Christian faith in the doctrine of the divine Incarnation

Appendix IV

Ecumenical Patriarchs of the Great Church of Christ

1.	St. Andrew the Apostle	Founder
2.	St. Stachys	38-54
3.	Onesimos	54-68
4.	Polycarp I	69-89
5.	Plutarch	89-105
6.	Sedekion	105-114
7.	Diogenes	114-129
8.	Eleutherios	129-136
9.	Felix	136-141
10.	Polycarp II	141-144
11.	Athenodoros	144-148
12.	Euzoios	148-154
13.	Laurentios	154-166
14.	Alypios	166-169
15.	Pertinex	169-187
16.	Olympianos	187-198
17.	Mark I	198-211
18.	Philadelphos	211-214
19.	Kyriakos I	214-230
20.	Kastinos	230-237
21.	Eugene I	237-242
22.	Titus	242-272
23.	Dometian	272-303
24.	Rufinos I	303
25.	Probos	303-315
26.	Metrophanes	315-325
27.	Alexander	325-340
28.	Paul I	340-341, 342-344, 348-350
29.	Eusebius of Nikomedia	341-342
30.	Makedonios I	342-348, 350-360
31.	Exodos	360-369
32.	Evagrios	369
33.	Demophilos	369-379

79.	Tarasios	784-806
80.	Nicephoros	806-815
81.	Theodotos I	815-821
82.	Antony I	821-832
83.	John VII	832-842
84.	Methodios I	842-846
85.	Ignatios I	846-857, 867-878
86.	Photios I	857-867, 878-886
87.	Stephen I	886-893
88.	Antony II	893-895
89.	Nicholas I	895-906, 911-925
90.	Euthymios I	906-911
91.	Stephen II	911-928
92.	Tryphon	928-931
93.	Theophylaktos	931-956
94.	Polyeuktos	956-970
95.	Basil I	970-974
96.	Anthony III	974-980
	Throne Vacant	*980-984*
97.	Nicholas II	984-995
98.	Sisinios II	995-998
99.	Sergios	999-1019
100.	Eustathios	1019-1025
101.	Alexios the Studite	1025-1043
102.	Michael I	1043-1058
103.	Constantine III	1059-1063
104.	John VIII	1064-1075
105.	Kosmas I	1075-1081
106.	Eustratios	1081-1084
107.	Nicholas III	1084-1111
108.	John IX	1111-1134
109.	Leo	1134-1143
110.	Michael II	1143-1146
111.	Kosmas II	1146-1147
112.	Nicholas IV	1147-1151
113.	Theodotos II	1151-1153
114.	Neophytos I	1153
115.	Constantine IV	1154-1156
116.	Luke	1156-1169
117.	Michael III	1169-1177
118.	Chariton	1177-1178
119.	Theodosios	1178-1183
120.	Basil II	1183-1187
121.	Niketas	1187-1190
122.	Leontios	1190-1191

166.	Maximos III	1476-1482
167.	Nephon II	1486-1489
168.	Maximos IV	1491-1497
169.	Joachim I	1498-1502, 1504-1505
170.	Pachomios	1503-1504, 1505-1514
171.	Theoleptos I	1514-1520
172.	Jeremiah I	1520-1522, 1523-1537, 1537-1545
173.	Joannikios I	1522-1523
174.	Dionysios II	1537, 1546-1555
175.	Joasaph II	1555-1565
176.	Metrophanes III	1565-1572, 1579-1580
177.	Jeremiah II	1572-1579, 1580-1584, 1585-1595
178.	Pachomios II	1584-1585
179.	Theoleptos II	1585-1586
180.	Matthew II	1595, 1599-1602
181.	Gabriel I	1596
182.	Theophanes I	1596-1597
183.	Meletios I	1597-1599
184.	Neophytos II	1602-1603, 1607-1612
185.	Raphael II	1603-1607
186.	Kyrillos I	1612, 1621-1623, 1623-1630, 1630-1634, 1634-1635, 1637-1638
187.	Timothy II	1612-1621
188.	Paul V	1622
189.	Anthimos II	1623
190.	Isaac	1630
191.	Kyrillos II	1634, 1635-1636, 1638-1639
192.	Athanasios III	1634, 1652
193.	Neophytos III	1636-1637
194.	Parthenios I	1639-1644
195.	Parthenios II	1644-1645, 1648-1651
196.	Joannicios II	1646-1648, 1651-1652, 1653-54, 1655-1656
197.	Kyrillos III	1652-1654
198.	Paisios I	1652-1653, 1654-1655
199.	Parthenios III	1656-1657
200.	Gabriel II	1657
201.	Theophanes II	1657
202.	Parthenios IV	1657-1662, 1665-1667, 1671
203.	Dionysios III	1662-1665
204.	Clement	1667
205.	Methodios III	1668-1671
206.	Dionysios IV	1671-1673, 1676-1679, 1683-1684, 1686-1687, 1693-1694
207.	Gerasimos II	1673-1675
208.	Athanasios IV	1679

254.	Joachim III	1878-1884, 1901-1912
255.	Joachim IV	1884-1887
256.	Dionysios VIII	1887-1891
257.	Neophytos VIII	1891-1894
258.	Anthimos VII	1895-1897
259.	Constantine V	1897-1901
260.	Germanos V	1913-1918
	Throne Vacant	*1918-1921*
261.	Meletios IV	1921-1923
262.	Gregory VII	1923-1924
263.	Constantine VI	1924-1925
264.	Basil III	1925-1929
265.	Photios II	1929-1935
266.	Benjamin	1936-1946
267.	Maximos V	1946-1948
268.	Athenagoras	1948-1972
269.	Dimitrios	1972-1991
270.	Bartholomew I	1991-present

Further Reading

Bartholomew (Ecumenical Patriarch), *Encountering the Mystery: Understanding Orthodox Christianity Today*, Doubleday: New York, 2008.

Clement, Olivier, *Conversations with Ecumenical Patriarch Bartholomew I*, St. Vladimir's Seminary Press: New York, 1997.

Geanakoplos, Deno, *A Short History of the Ecumenical Patriarchate of Constantinople (330-1990): "First Among Equals" in the Eastern Orthodox Church*, Holy Cross Press: Brookline, 1990.

Istavridis, Vasil, *History of the Ecumenical Patriarchate: Bibliography*, vol. 2, Kyriakidis Publications: Thessaloniki, 2004. [Foreword in Greek; sources in Greek and English]

Maximos, Metropolitan of Sardes, *The Oecumenical Patriarchate in the Orthodox Church: A Study in the History and the Canons of the Church*, Patriarchal Institute of Patristic Studies: Thessaloniki, 1976.

Oecumenical Patriarchate: The Great Church of Christ, ed. Athanasios Paliouras, Orthodox Centre of the Ecumenical Patriarchate: Geneva; E. Tzaphere: Athens, 1989. [Collected essays in Greek]

Pelikan, Jaroslav, *The Christian Tradition: A History of the Development of Doctrine*, Chicago University Press: Chicago, 1971-1989, 5 volumes.

Runciman, Steven, *Fall of Constantinople, 1453*, Cambridge University Press: Cambridge, 1990.

Runciman, Steven, *The Great Church in Captivity: A Study of the Patriarchate of Constantinople from the Eve of the Turkish Conquest to the Greek War of Independence*, Cambridge University Press: London, 1968.

Ware, Kallistos (Bishop of Diokleia), *The Orthodox Church*, 2nd rev. ed., Penguin Books: London, 1993.

Chryssavgis, John, *Light Through Darkness: The Orthodox Spiritual Tradition*, Darton Longman and Todd: London UK; Orbis Books: Maryknoll NY, 2004.